Hernán Cortés

Discover The Life Of An Explorer

Trish Kline

Rourke

Publishing LLC

Vero Beach, Florida 32964

www.rourkepublishing.com

PHOTO CREDITS: IRC-www.historypictures.com: cover, title page, pages 4, 7, 8, 12, 13, 15, 17, 18; © Painet, Inc.: page 21; © Artville: page 10.

Title page: The Aztec believed Hernán Cortés was a god.

Editor: Frank Sloan

Cover design by Nicola Stratford

Library of Congress Cataloging-in-Publication Data

Kline, Trish
    Hernán Cortés / Trish Kline.
       p. cm. — (Discover the life of an explorer)
    Summary: Introduces the life of Hernán Cortés, the spanish explorer who discovered Baja California and explored the Pacific coast of Mexico, but who is best remembered for conquering the Aztec Empire.
    Includes bibliographical references and index.
    ISBN 1-58952-293-1
    1. Cortés, Hernán, 1485-1547—Juvenile literature. 2. Mexico—History—Conquest, 1519-1540—Juvenile literature. 3. Mexico—Discovery and exploration—Spanish—Juvenile literature. 4. Explorers—Mexico—Biography—Juvenile literature. 5. Explorers—Spain—Biography—Juvenile literature. [1. Cortés, Hernando, 1485-1547. 2. Explorers. 3. Mexico—History—Conquest, 1519-1540.] I. Title.

F1230.C835 K65 2002
972'02'092—dc21
[B]
                                       2002020709

Printed in the USA

CG/CG

TABLE OF CONTENTS

LONGING FOR ADVENTURE

Hernán Cortés (hair NAHN cor TEZ) was born in Spain in 1485. He went to school but was not a good student. He wanted adventure. He read about voyages to the New World. He wanted to find gold and riches. In 1511, he sailed to the New World.

Cortés sailed to the New World in search of adventure.

5

BUILDING AN ARMY

In 1518, the governor of present-day Cuba sent Cortés on an **expedition**. He wanted Cortés to go to the land we now know as Mexico. The governor wanted Cortés to claim the land for Spain.

But Cortés wanted to do more. He had heard stories of gold and silver. Cortés began to build an army. He bought guns, **cannons**, and horses.

The governor became worried that Cortés would not follow his orders. He told Cortés not to go. Cortés went anyway.

Cortés hoped to find riches in the New World.

A GREAT EMPIRE

The Aztec Indians lived in Mexico. **Tenochtitlán** was the capital city of their **empire**. It was a very large city. More than 300,000 people lived there. It was larger and more beautiful than any city in Spain.

Cortés's small army was no match for such a great empire. But luck was on his side.

Tenochtitlán was more beautiful than any city Cortés had ever seen.

PACIFIC
OCEAN

NEW SPAIN

Tenochtitlan

GULF OF
MEXICO

The Aztecs believed in a god named **Quetzalcoatl**. The Aztecs believed this god created man. Very long ago, the god had visited the Aztec people. He promised to return someday. The Aztecs waited hopefully for the return of their god.

The Aztecs had dark skin. The god they waited for had light skin and wore a beard.

Tenochtitlán was the center of the Aztec empire.

Montezuma ruled the Aztec empire.

Cortés and his men sometimes used force to control the Aztecs.

A GOD RETURNS

Cortés had light skin and had a beard. The Aztec ruler **Montezuma** believed Cortés was their god. Montezuma welcomed Cortés into the city. He gave him gold and other riches.

Cortés's soldiers walked about the city. They found gold in the temples. They took the gold for themselves. The soldiers also killed many Aztecs. The Aztecs thought that gods should not act this way.

The Aztec ruler welcomed Cortés and his soldiers.

THE END OF AN EMPIRE

Cortés asked Montezuma to talk to the Aztecs. The ruler tried to stop the attack. The Aztecs would not listen. They threw stones at the ruler. Three days later, the ruler died. Cortés and his army were chased out of the city.

A year later, Cortés returned. He brought more soldiers. He had many guns and cannons. For three months, Cortés's army attacked the city. Finally, the Aztecs **surrendered**.

Aztec warriors defended their city, but they were defeated.

BUILDING ANOTHER GREAT CITY

Cortés built present-day Mexico City on top of the **ruins** of the Aztec capital. Soon, people arrived from Spain to live in the new city.

Cortés had taken great riches and gold from the Aztecs. The king of Spain was very happy. Cortés was made the governor of New Spain. He died in 1547. He was 62 years old.

The king of Spain made Cortés governor of the Aztec land.

CORTÉS AND THE AZTEC EMPIRE

Cortés went on many other expeditions. He discovered present-day Baja California in northwest Mexico. He also explored the Pacific coast of Mexico.

However, Hernán Cortés is best remembered as the explorer who **conquered** the Aztec Empire.

Cortés found adventure, riches, and power in the New World.

IMPORTANT DATES TO REMEMBER

1485	Born in Spain
1511	Sailed to the New World
1518	Sent on expedition to present-day Mexico
1519	Aztecs surrendered to Cortés's army
1547	Died at age 62

GLOSSARY

cannons (KAN enz) — large weapons used in war

conquered (KONG kerd) — to overcome by force

empire (EM pyre) — a large kingdom or nation

expedition (EK spi dish en) — to be sent on a journey

Montezuma (MONT eh ZOOM uh) — leader of the Aztecs

Quetzalcoatl (KET sal KWAT uhl) — an Aztec god

ruins (ROO ins) — the remains of something that has been destroyed

surrendered (se REN derd) — gave up

Tenochtitlán (TEN notch tee TLAN) — the capital city of the Aztec empire

INDEX

Further Reading

Crisfield, Deborah. *The Travels of Hernan Cortes*. Raintree Steck-Vaughn, 2000.
De Angelis, Gina. *Hernando Cortes and the Conquest of Mexico*. Chelsea House
   Publishing, 2000.

Websites To Visit

http://www.encarta.com
http://www.pbs.org
http://www.mariner.org   (The Mariner's Museum, Newport News, VA)

About The Author

Trish Kline has written a great number of nonfiction books for the school and library market. Her publishing credits include two dozen books, as well as hundreds of newspaper and magazine articles, anthologies, short stories, poetry, and plays. She lives in Helena, Montana.